The House That Jane Built

A STORY ABOUT
Jane Addams

TANYA LEE STONE

ILLUSTRATED BY KATHRYN BROWN

Christy Ottaviano Books

HENRY HOLT AND COMPANY • NEW YORK

For my father, A. Harris Stone, whose openness to the world is a thing of beauty,
and who showed me, by example, the importance of community and how to create it.
And for Sarah Aronson, who embraces inclusivity and community in everything she does.

—T. L. S.

For Sandy Staub

—K. B.

Kathryn Brown wishes to thank the Jane Addams Hull-House Museum, UIC University Library,
the Sophia Smith Collection and Neilson Library at Smith College, W.E.B. Du Bois Library at UMass,
Northampton Forbes Library, Hartford Public Library, Christy Ottaviano, and Tanya Lee Stone.

Henry Holt and Company, LLC, *Publishers since 1866*
120 Broadway, New York, NY 10271
mackids.com

Library of Congress Cataloging-in-Publication Data
Stone, Tanya Lee.
The house that Jane built : a story about Jane Addams / Tanya Lee Stone ;
illustrated by Kathryn Brown. — First edition.
pages   cm
"Christy Ottaviano books."
Includes bibliographical references.
ISBN 978-0-8050-9049-9 (hardcover)
1. Addams, Jane, 1860–1935—Juvenile literature. 2. Hull House (Chicago, Ill.)—Juvenile literature. 3. Women social workers—United States—Biography—Juvenile literature.
4. Women social reformers—United States—Biography—Juvenile literature. 5. Chicago (Ill.)—Social conditions—20th century—Juvenile literature. I. Brown, Kathryn, 1955– illustrator. II. Title.
HV40.32.A33S76 2015   361.92—dc23 [B]   2014036098

First Edition—2015 / Designed by April Ward
The illustrations were rendered in watercolor and pen and ink on watercolor paper.
Photographs courtesy of Jane Addams Hull-House Museum, University of Illinois at Chicago.

Printed in China by RR Donnelley Asia Printing Solutions Ltd., Dongguan City, Guangdong Province

9   10   8

A house stands on a busy street
Its doors are opened wide,
To all who come it bids good cheer,
To some it says, Abide.

—JANE ADDAMS

In 1889, a wealthy young woman named Jane Addams moved into a lovely, elegant house in Chicago, Illinois. But instead of moving into a lovely, elegant neighborhood, she picked a house that was smack in the middle of one of the filthiest, poorest parts of town.

Why would a wealthy young woman do this when she could have lived anywhere?

Jane was just six years old when she went on a trip with her father and noticed that not everyone lived like her family did. She vowed that one day she would live "right in the midst of horrid little houses" and find a way to fix the world.

Jane was a strong soul from the start. And she was
brave. When she and her stepbrother George were
young, they would sneak away at night to explore in
nearby caves. Once, Jane lowered George over a cliff
on a rope to spy on an owl in its nest.

Jane was smart. She read and
read from her father's book collection,
which doubled as the town library.
Most girls did not go to college then,
but Jane's father believed women
should be educated. She went to
Rockford Female Seminary and
graduated at the top of her class.

But when school was over, she
wasn't sure what to do with her life.
That same summer, her father died.
Jane was lost.

About two years later, she and her friends traveled to Europe. They went to the theater, the opera, and many beautiful places. But then Jane saw something in London she couldn't forget: people in ragged clothes with outstretched hands, begging a cart vendor to buy his leftover rotten fruits and vegetables that hadn't sold at market. The spoiled food was all they could afford.

What could she do to help? Long after her trip was over, the question stuck in her mind. She remembered how she felt when she was six.

Jane traveled back to London to learn about a place she had heard was helping the poor in a brand-new way. At Toynbee Hall, the idea was to have rich and poor people live together in the same community and learn from each other. Instead of simply serving soup, for example, people could take cooking classes. Other skills were taught as well.

Toynbee Hall was the first settlement house. It was called a settlement house because the well-off people who worked there during the day didn't go back to their own homes at night. Instead, they "settled" in and lived at Toynbee Hall, right in the same neighborhood as the needy.

Jane now knew what to do.

She told her friend Ellen Gates Starr about her plan to build a settlement house in Chicago. It was "as if a racehorse had burst out of the gate, free at last to pour every ounce of energy into running."

There was a glittery side to Chicago, with its mansions, fancy shops, and sparkling lakefront. But there was a gritty side, too. One million people lived in Chicago in 1889. Most were immigrants—people who came from other countries. They came for a better life, but they didn't speak English. That made it hard to find good jobs. Many needed help.

Jane found the perfect house. It had big rooms with high ceilings and marble fireplaces. And it was in one of the worst neighborhoods in the city. Garbage lay rotting in the streets, piled high. Large families were crammed into tiny, ramshackle houses with no running water. The smell from back-lot outhouses hung in the air. Rough boys ran the streets, stirring up trouble because they had nothing to do.

The house had belonged to Charles J. Hull, and he had left it to a wealthy cousin named Helen Culver. At first, Jane paid rent, but after she told Helen what she had in mind, Helen gave her the house for free. In thanks, Jane named it Hull House.

Jane moved in on September 18, 1889. The very first night, she was so busy and excited that she forgot to lock a side door before going to sleep. But no one broke in. She decided to leave Hull House unlocked from then on so people would know they could come in at any time.

People who didn't have enough to eat or had no shoes on their feet or had just lost a job began to find their way to Hull House.

Of course, it wasn't always peaceful. Once, a couple of boys threw rocks at the house and broke a window.

Instead of getting upset, Jane took it as a sign to give the neighborhood kids something to do. She had her own way of looking at things.

Another time, Jane discovered a man in the house looking for something to steal. He tried to jump out a window to escape, but she showed him the door so he wouldn't get hurt. When he broke in a second time, she asked him why. He said he was out of work and had no money. Jane told him to report back the next morning. When he did, she gave him a job.

Jane spent her own money running Hull House, and asked other well-off people to donate, too. She did not want to be paid for working there. Even when people gave her gifts, she gave them away. Her friends teased Jane about this. One friend gave her new underwear with her initials just so Jane couldn't pass them on. But she did!

Any problem Jane discovered, she tackled. No running water in houses meant no easy way to bathe. This led to sickness. So Jane put in a public bath. People flocked to it, which helped her convince city officials they needed to build more public baths.

No safe place for children to play? Jane talked a wealthy man into giving her the lot he owned near Hull House. Workmen tore down the shabby buildings and turned the lot into a playground. It was the first one in Chicago!

Little kids home alone because their parents had to work fourteen hours a day? Jane started a morning kindergarten and after-school clubs. She also set up afternoon classes for older kids who had to go to work during the school day.

Jane did not do all this alone. Ellen Gates Starr was her partner from the start. Many other smart, generous people moved into Hull House and helped. They taught literature, art, English, math, science, and cooking.

Soon there was not just one building, but two. Then three, and four, and more. By 1907, Hull House had grown into thirteen buildings, including a gymnasium, coffee house, theatre, music school, community kitchen, and an art gallery.

ACT WELL YOUR PART, THERE ALL THE HONOUR LIES.

By the early 1920s, more than nine thousand people a week visited Hull House. The house that Jane built brought all kinds of people together and helped those in need. It changed a bad neighborhood into a great and strong community. Hull House transformed the lives of all who stepped inside.

Today, every community center in America, in large part, has Jane Addams to thank. With all that she did, both inside and outside the house that Jane built, her childhood wish to help fix the world came true.

Author's Note: A Little Bit More

There is much more to know about Jane Addams than could possibly fit in a picture book. I have included some additional information here, but I urge readers to explore other books about this remarkable woman.

Addams was known not only for her work at Hull House, but also for speaking out against war and for being a peace  activist. During World War I, she co-founded the Woman's Peace Party and was elected its president. She was then invited to an international peace meeting in April 1915, during which the Women's International League for Peace and Freedom (WILPF) was formed, with Jane at its head. She and a few female colleagues traveled

Jane Addams around age eight.

throughout war-torn Europe and witnessed firsthand the violence and suffering caused by war.

For the next fifteen years, in addition to her role at Hull House, she traveled the world and spoke out against war. Her opinions were not always popular. The Federal Bureau of Investigation (FBI) kept a file on her, and she was called "the most dangerous woman in America." But none of that stopped her. In 1931, she became the first American woman to win the Nobel Peace Prize.

Addams wrote hundreds of articles in her lifetime as well as

Jane Addams in 1891.

eleven books. She worked for the women's suffrage movement, advised several presidents, and was a founding member of both the National Association for the Advancement of Colored People (NAACP) and the American Civil Liberties Union (ACLU).

By 1900, Jane Addams was one of the most famous women in the world. Tourists visited Hull House in hopes of catching sight of her. She was a bona fide celebrity! She died on May 21, 1935, at the age of seventy-four. In Chicago, thousands paid respect to her at Hull House. All over the world, people mourned her death and celebrated her extraordinary life.

Until 2012, the programs at the Jane Addams Hull House Association in Chicago had helped thousands of people a year. Two of the original Hull House buildings have been preserved and turned into the Jane Addams Hull-House Museum. There are many wonderful exhibits, including Jane Addams's bedroom, where her personal diary, childhood drawings, and Nobel Peace Prize are on display. This organization is dedicated to carrying on the work that Jane Addams began at Hull House more than 120 years ago.

Jane Addams with schoolchildren on the steps of the residents' dining hall at Hull House, circa 1934.

Jane Addams with neighborhood Mexican, Jewish, and Italian children at the Mary Crane Nursery, circa 1935.

Sources

Addams, Jane. *Twenty Years at Hull-House.* New York: Macmillan, 1910.

Ferris, Helen. *When I Was a Girl: The Stories of Five Famous Women as Told by Themselves.* New York: Junior Literary Guild, 1930.

Fradin, Judith Bloom, and Dennis Brindell Fradin. *Jane Addams: Champion of Democracy.* New York: Clarion Books, 2006.

Johnson, Mary Ann, ed., and Wallace Kirkland. *The Many Faces of Hull-House: The Photographs of Wallace Kirkland.* Urbana: University of Illinois Press, 1989.

Knight, Louise W. *Jane Addams: Spirit in Action.* New York: W. W. Norton & Company, 2010.

———. *Citizen: Jane Addams and the Struggle for Democracy.* Chicago: University of Chicago Press, 2006.

Linn, James Weber. *Jane Addams: A Biography.* New York: D. Appleton-Century Company, 1935.

Polacheck, Hilda Satt. *I Came a Stranger: The Story of a Hull-House Girl.* Urbana: University of Illinois Press, 1989.

Stebner, Eleanor J. *The Women of Hull House: A Study in Spirituality, Vocation, and Friendship.* New York: State University of New York Press, 1997.

Source Notes

"A house stands on a busy street . . .": Fradin and Fradin, p. 71.

"right in the midst of horrid little houses": Linn, p. 27.

"as if a racehorse had burst out of the gate . . .": Knight, *Jane Addams: Spirit in Action*, p. 65.